for Mum

TOMMY'S CHRISTMAS TUN

Traditional carols and popular Christmas tunes for the you. joy. Words to the tunes are also given so that family and friends ca. and the Christmas tree!

This selection, easily sung in the home or classroom, is written for the young violinist while still being playable by other instruments.

Colour in the drawings and have fun with Tommy's Quiz, his Memory Tune and lots more!

Chosen and adapted by Joyce McIver
Drawings by Andrew Magee
Published by Cute Cats Music 1999

Other books in the series:
Tommy's Scottish Tunes (September 1999)
Tommy's Burns Tunes (December 1999)

ISBN 0 9536433 1 X

Dear Young Music Maker,

Hello, I'm very pleased to meet you!

My name is Tommy McTavish and I come from Falkland, a wee village in Fife, in the east of Scotland.

I just love to play and sing my tunes. Sometimes I play and my friends sing. Sometimes I play and my family sing.

Sometimes I practise very hard on my own! But I always have great fun!

I hope *you* have great fun learning all my Christmas tunes!

Look out for my paw prints – they might help you! Happy playing and happy singing! Lots of love,

Tommy

CONTENTS

Here is my very own tune - I hope you like it! You can play it or sing it as a round.
Start each part at my paw print.

Tommy's Own Tune

Joyce McIver

Tommy says "If you can, with your pencil please, carefully name the notes of this tune.
Start at my single paw print. (Ignore the letters above the notes - they are for a piano or guitar accompaniment.)"

Tune 1

Jingle Bells

Traditional

Jingle bells, jingle bells,
Jingle all the way,
Oh what fun it is to ride
In a one horse open sleigh,

Jingle bells, jingle bells,
Jingle all the way,
Oh what fun it is to ride
In a one horse open sleigh.

Tommy says "Try naming the notes again on the straight line (pencil only, please!), and notice all the repeat signs."

Tune 2

Little Donkey

Words & music by Eric Boswell

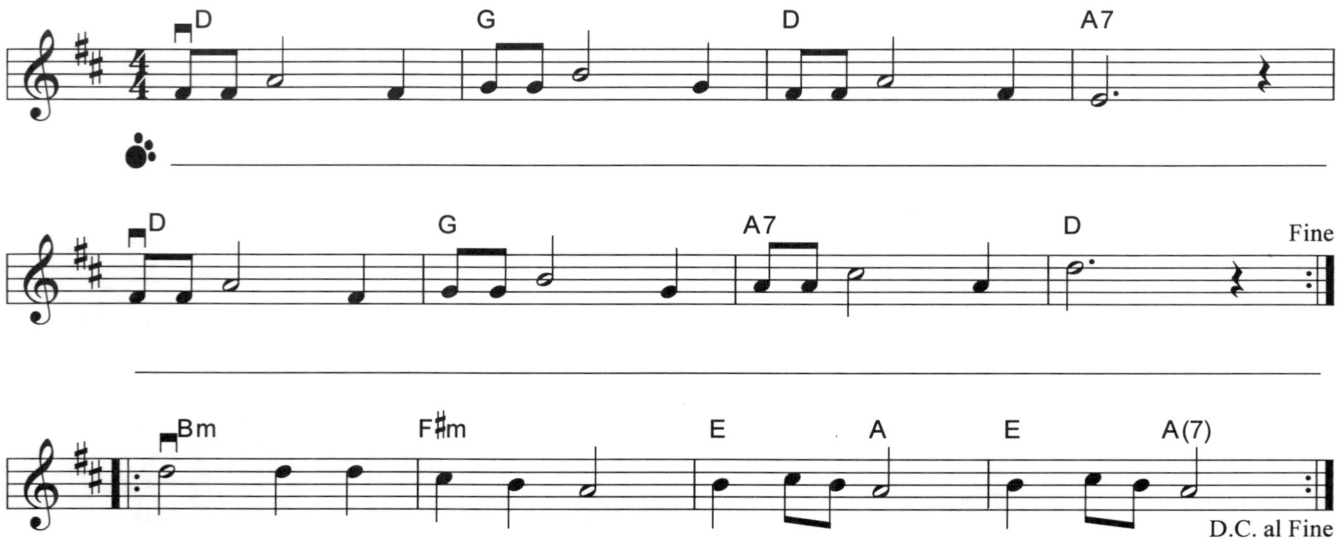

Little donkey, little donkey,
On the dusty road.
Got to keep on plodding onwards,
With your precious load.

Been a long time, little donkey,
Through the winter's night.
Don't give up now, little donkey,
Bethlehem's in sight.

Ring out those bells tonight,
Bethlehem, Bethlehem.
Follow that star tonight,
Bethlehem, Bethlehem.

Little donkey, little donkey,
Had a heavy day.
Little donkey, carry Mary
Safely on her way.

Tommy's Tip for violinists "Carefully move your second finger on D across to the G string for the two B notes."

Tune 3

The Holly and the Ivy

Traditional

The holly and the ivy,
When they are both full grown,
Of all the trees that are in the wood,
The holly bears the crown.

The rising of the sun,
And the running of the deer,
The playing of the merry organ,
Sweet singing in the choir.

Tommy's Tip "Watch out for all the long four beat notes - count 1 2 3 4 in your head!"

Tune 4 — Rudolph the Red-Nosed Reindeer

Words & music by Johnny Marks

Rudolph, the red-nosed reindeer had a very shiny nose;
And if you ever saw it, you would even say it glows.
All of the other reindeer used to laugh and call him names,
They never let poor Rudolph join in any reindeer games.

Then one foggy Christmas Eve, Santa came to say:
"Rudolph, with your nose so bright, won't you guide my sleigh tonight."
Then how the reindeer loved him as they shouted out with glee:
"Rudolph, the red-nosed reindeer, you'll go down in history!"

Tommy's Tip "Play and sing this tune very gently - in verse one Jesus is asleep on the hay. (Violinists, watch out for the C♮s)"

Tune 5

Away in a Manger

Traditional

Away in a manger, no crib for a bed,
The little Lord Jesus laid down his sweet head.
The stars in the bright sky looked down where he lay,
The little Lord Jesus asleep on the hay.

The cattle are lowing, the baby awakes,
But little Lord Jesus no crying he makes,
I love thee, Lord Jesus, look down from the sky,
And stay by my side until morning is nigh.

Be near me, Lord Jesus, I ask thee to stay
Close by me for ever, and love me, I pray:
Bless all the dear children in thy tender care,
And fit us for heaven, to live with thee there.

Tommy says "With your pencil, practise neatly naming the notes again - I hope it's easier now!"

Tune 6 — Good King Wenceslas

Traditional

Good King Wenceslas looked out,
On the feast of Stephen,
When the snow lay round about,
Deep, and crisp, and even;
Brightly shone the moon that night,
Though the frost was cruel,
When a poor man came in sight,
Gath'ring winter fuel.

Tommy's Tip for violinists "Watch out for the slurs. Sail your bow over the strings!"

Tune 7

I Saw Three Ships

Traditional

I saw three ships come sailing in,
On Christmas Day, on Christmas Day.
I saw three ships come sailing in,
On Christmas Day in the morning.

And what was in those ships all three?
On Christmas Day, on Christmas Day.
And what was in those ships all three?
On Christmas Day in the morning.

Our Saviour Christ and his lady.
On Christmas Day, on Christmas Day.
Our Saviour Christ and his lady.
On Christmas Day in the morning.

And all the bells on earth shall ring,
On Christmas Day, on Christmas Day
And all the bells on earth shall ring,
On Christmas Day in the morning.

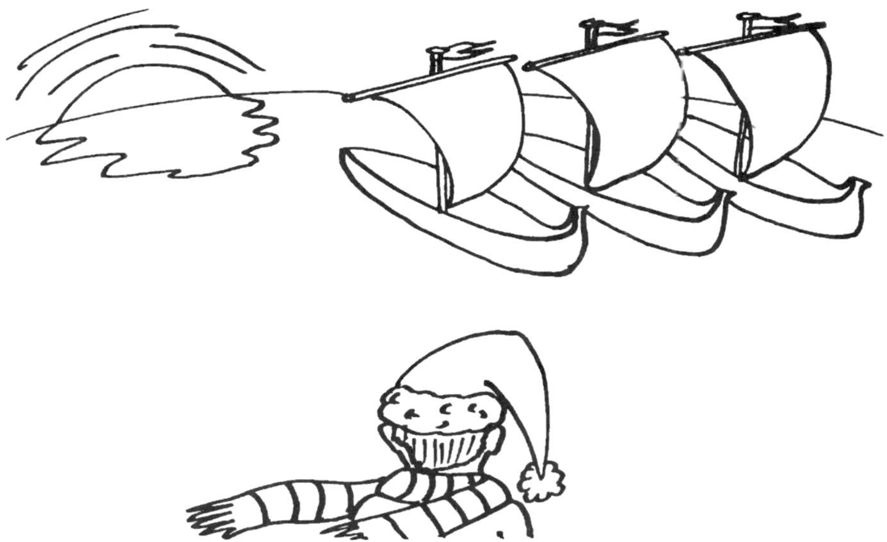

Tommy's Tip. "When you reach the bottom of the page be careful to go back to the fancy sign. Violinists, take care with all the slurs."

Tune 8 O Little Town of Bethlehem

Traditional

O little town of Bethlehem,
How still we see thee lie!
Above thy deep and dreamless sleep
The silent stars go by.
Yet in thy dark streets shineth
The everlasting light;
The hopes and fears of all the years
Are met in thee tonight.

Tommy says "This is a German carol. The words we use are a translation. Play the rhythm smoothly - you play it ______ times!?"

Tune 9

Still the Night

Traditional

Still the night, holy the night!
Sleeps the world; hid from sight,
Mary and Joseph in stable bare
Watch o'er the Child beloved and fair
Sleeping in heavenly rest,
Sleeping in heavenly rest.

Still the night, holy the night!
Shepherds first saw the light,
Heard resounding clear and long,
Far and near the angel-song,
"Christ the Redeemer is here!"
"Christ the Redeemer is here!"

Still the night, holy the night!
Son of God, O how bright
Love is smiling from thy face!
Strikes for us now the hour of grace,
Saviour, since thou art born!
Saviour, since thou art born!

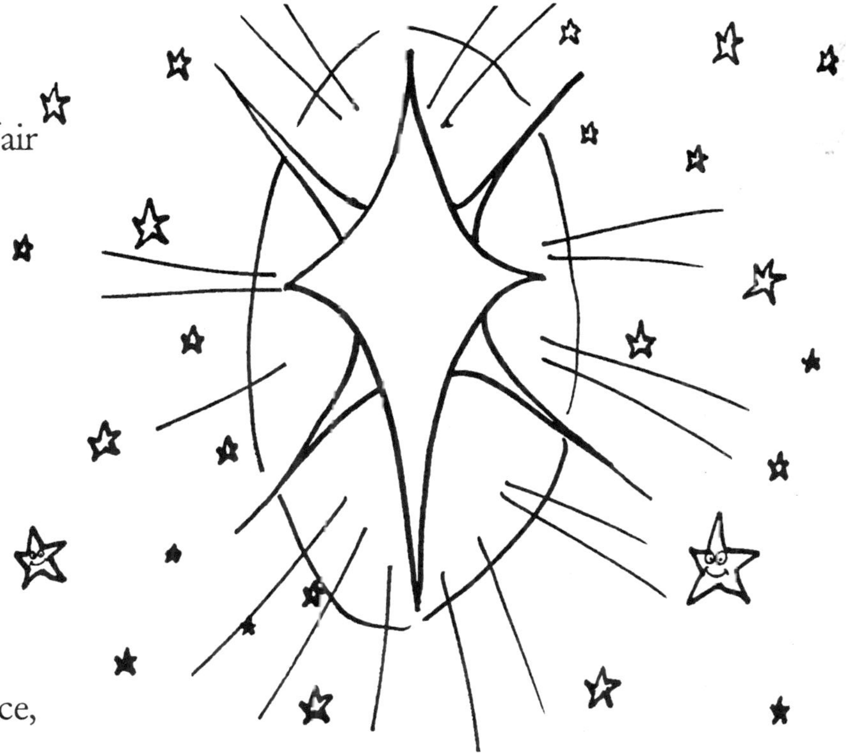

"This is a very happy tune - I love it! It is my Christmas Memory Tune. This means I can play it without looking at the music. Carefully learn the tune and see if you can play or sing it by memory. Good luck and keep trying!" Tommy

---

Tune 10 We Wish You a Merry Christmas

Traditional

We wish you a Merry Christmas,
We wish you a Merry Christmas,
We wish you a Merry Christmas,
And a Happy New Year.

Now bring us some figgy pudding,
Now bring us some figgy pudding,
Now bring us some figgy pudding,
And bring some out here.

For we all like figgy pudding,
We all like figgy pudding,
For we all like figgy pudding,
So bring some out here.

And we won't go till we've got some,
We won't go till we've got some,
And we won't go till we've got some,
So bring some out here.

Repeat verse 1

I played this tune by memory today!
(date)__________________

Tommy's Quiz

Tommy wonders what you've discovered about the music and the tunes in this book. Check with your teacher if you've got all the answers right. Good luck!

1. What is the name of the town where "the silent stars go by"? ____________________
2. ♯ What is this called? ________________
3. Who was the baby "asleep on the hay"? ____________________
4. In musical language what does **FINE** mean? ____________________
5. What do "we all like" to eat? ______________________________________
6. How many tunes use the repeat sign? (𝄆) _______________
7. Who "looked out" one night, when the moon was shining brightly? ________________
8. How many tunes have three beats in each bar? ($\frac{3}{4}$ time) _______________________
9. Describe the weather on the night Rudolph guided Santa's sleigh ________________
10. Which tune is the Memory Tune? Can you play it by memory yet? _________________

"Well done! See you soon," Love Tommy.